**Other books by the author**

**Le Dragon qui ne voulait
plus manger les enfants**
Édition Paris Nathan 1985
Auteure Henriette Bichonnier
Illustrateur Daniel Guerrier

**Fahr Mit !**
l'allemand à l'école élémentaire
Édition Paris Nathan 1991

**Le Loto en dix leçons**
Édition Paris Hachette 1977

**OK !**
4e. seconde langue
Édition Paris Nathan 1985

**OK !**
3e. seconde langue
Édition Paris Nathan 1985

**Où est l'erreur ?**
Tomes 1, 2, 3
Édition Paris Nathan 2003

**Où est l'erreur ?**
Édition France Loisirs 2004

**Transfert "panoramique"**
Édition Paris Lito 2003

**¿ Dónde está el error ?**
Édition San Pablo Madrid 2007

**Find fejlen!**
Borgen édition 2004
Danemark, Suède, Norvège

**Où est l'erreur?**
Tomato House 2007
RPC

**Où est l'erreur?**
Changpo desing group 2007
Corée

**¿ Dónde está el error ?**
Larousse édition 2006
Mexique, Argentine, Chili

**Encyclopédie Dokéo**
Collectif d'auteurs
Édition Paris Nathan 2005

Waldo D. Guerrier

Where's the mistake?

# Spot the nonsense

SPOT
EDITION

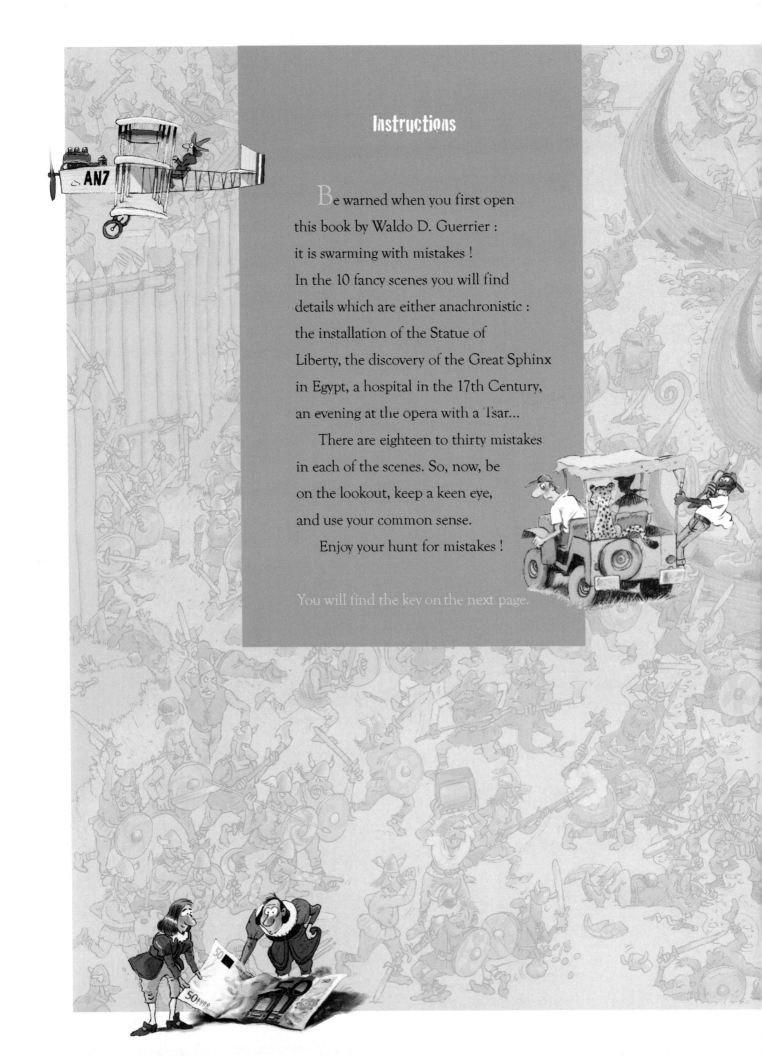

## Instructions

Be warned when you first open
this book by Waldo D. Guerrier :
it is swarming with mistakes !
In the 10 fancy scenes you will find
details which are either anachronistic :
the installation of the Statue of
Liberty, the discovery of the Great Sphinx
in Egypt, a hospital in the 17th Century,
an evening at the opera with a Tsar...

There are eighteen to thirty mistakes
in each of the scenes. So, now, be
on the lookout, keep a keen eye,
and use your common sense.

Enjoy your hunt for mistakes !

You will find the key on the next page.

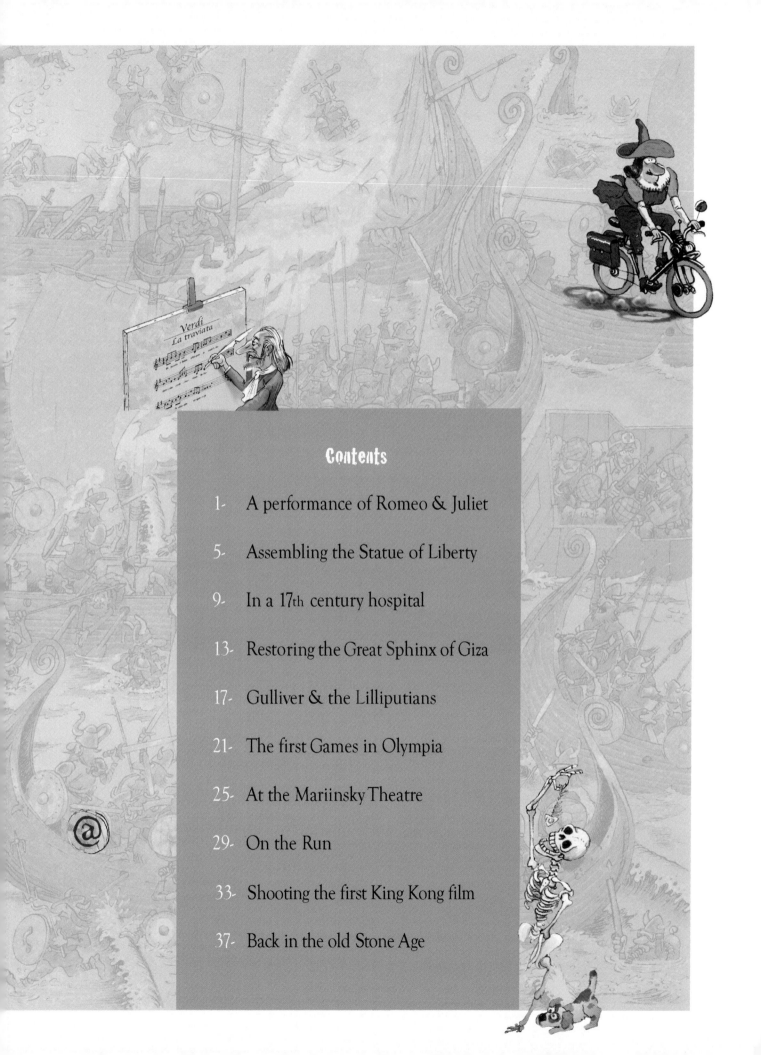

# Contents

A performance of
# Romeo and Juliet
by Shakespeare's company
in London circa 1595

William Shakespeare (1564 -1616) was an English poet playwright, and actor, widely regarded as the greatest writer in the English language and the world's pre-eminent dramatist. He is often called England's national poet.

He started his career as an actor and with his company performed in the various London theatres, also called playhouses.

The public theatres were three stories high, and built around an open (roofless) space at the centre. Usually polygonal in plan to give an overall rounded effect, the three levels of inward-facing galleries overlooked the open centre, into which jutted the stage—essentially a platform surrounded on three sides by the audience, only the rear being restricted for the entrances and exits of the actors and seating for the musicians.

**Romeo and Juliet** is a tragedy written by William Shakespeare early in the early 1590s, about two young star-crossed lovers whose deaths ultimately reconcile their feuding families.

It was among Shakespeare's most popular plays during his lifetime and, along with **Hamlet**, is one of his most frequently performed plays. Today, the title characters are regarded as archetypal young lovers.

Please turn over and spot 19 mistakes

②

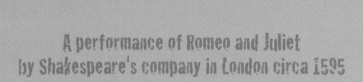

## A performance of Romeo and Juliet
by Shakespeare's company in London circa 1595

# Key

1- Spotlights

2- Two advertising posters

3- A CCTV camera

4- Binoculars on a tripod

5- A machinist hoovering the stage

6- A mountain bike on the stage

7- A serviceman

8- Loudspeakers

9- A fire extinguisher

10- A camera

11- An actor with a Greek theater mask

12- An electric guitar

13- A microphone

14- An Indian Kathakali dancer

15- The prompter's box is oriented towards the audience (a prompter is a person hidden from the audience who reminds actors of their lines if they are forgotten)

16- A lifebuoy

17- An air hostess

18- An umbrella

19- A jockey on a race horse

# Assembling
# the Statue of Liberty
## in New York Harbor 1885-86

To honor its friendship with America, France gave the U.S. a special gift: sculptor Frederic-Auguste Bartholdi's beautiful statue called Liberty Enlightening the World.

The Statue of Liberty arrived in New York Harbor on June 19, 1885. It came in 350 pieces packed into 214 crates. It was assembled on a pedestal base built by the United States. The 151-foot tall Statue was dedicated on October 28, 1886

The Statue represents Libertas, the Roman goddess of freedom. She holds a torch in one hand and a tablet inscribed with the date of the Declaration of Independence in the other.

Built in France, the Statue is made of hundreds of thin copper sheets assembled on a frame of steel supports. The outer layer of the statue is copper that's only 3/32 of an inch thick — the thickness of two pennies put together. Nevertheless, the Statue is very strong : The inner framework was engineered and designed by Gustave Eiffel, who built the Eiffel Tower.

The frame allows the Statue of Liberty to move with changes in temperature and wind speed. It also allowed staircases to be built on the inside of the Statue.

When the Statue was originally assembled, it was a dull brown color, reflecting the natural color of its copper plates. Over the next 30 years, though, it slowly turned to green.

The Statue alone stands 151 feet tall. The pedestal stands 154 feet tall, making the top of the torch 305 feet above ground level.

The Statue contains 62,000 pounds of copper and 250,000 pounds of steel. The concrete pedestal weighs 54 million pounds. Winds of 50 miles per hour can cause the Statue to sway up to 3 inches and the torch up to 6 inches.

**Please turn over and spot 29 mistakes**

(5)

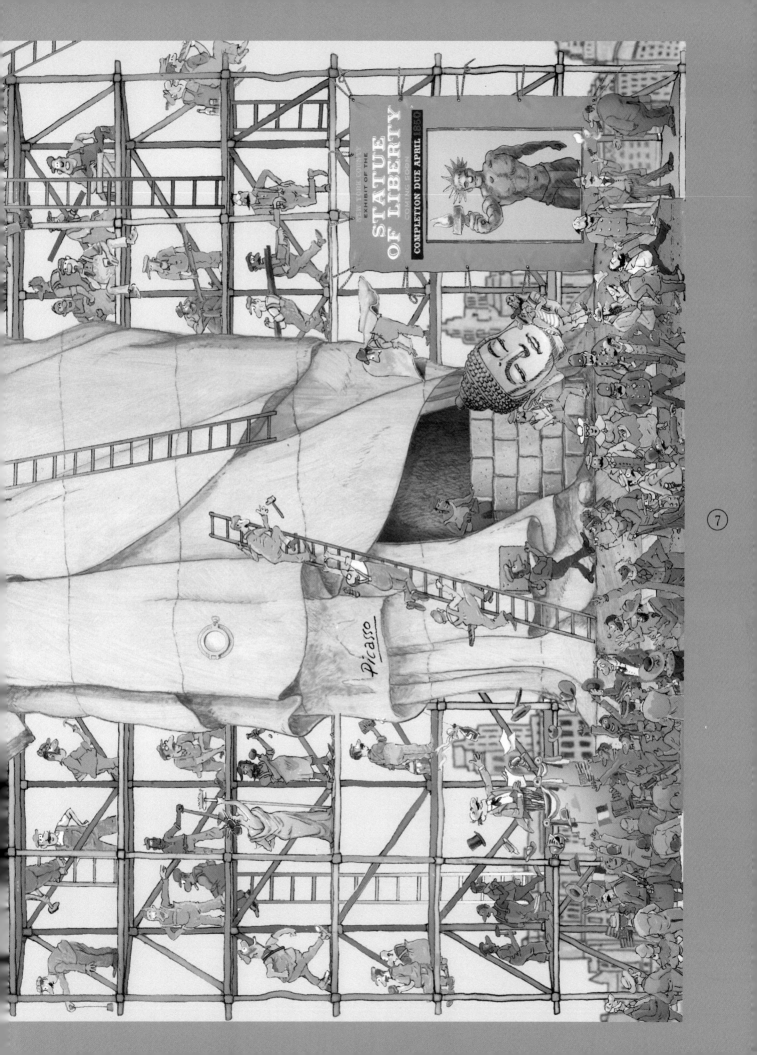

Assembling the Statue of Liberty in New York Harbor 1885-86

Key

1- A helicopter

2- The Statue should hold a torch

3- The Concord supersonic jetliner

4- An ad on the airship

5- The Statue should raise her right arm instead of her left

6- There should be 7 points (7 seas and 7 continents) on her crown, not 8

7- She wears a hoop earring

8- She wears sunglasses

9- A talkie-walkie

10- Egyptian slaves pushing a stone block

11- There is a mountain climber

12- The Statue holds a copy of Mad Magazine (founded 1952)

13- A barcode (developed in 1952, used only from 1973)

14- The statue was originally a dull brown color. Its green colour came gradually from the natural oxidation of the copper plates. And of course no one painted it !

15- A porthole

16- Artist Auguste Bartholdi sculpting the Statue (it wasn't sculpted but made of thin copper sheets assembled on a frame)

17- His model is holding a broom instead of a torch

18- The foot of the painter's ladder is resting on thin air

19- The Statue is signed "Picasso" instead of "Bartholdi"

20- On the poster the date for completion is wrong

21- The Statue on the poster shows the Colossus of Rhodes, a huge ancient Greek statue from which the word "colossal" is derived

22- The President is inaugurating the Statue whereas the works are not over

23- There is tomato sauce instead of champagne for the dedication ceremonial

24- There is a modern microphone (in those days microphones, invented by Emile Berliner in 1877, were not mobile)

25- There is a medieval helm among the hats thrown in the air

26- Women and people of color were not invited to the dedication ceremony

27- The frame designed by Bartholdi to support the statue was made of steel and not of stone, as architect Viollet-le-Duc had suggested

28- The Buddha head is out of place here

29- "Made in China" is printed on her left arm

In 17th Century Europe, medical care was still mostly supplied by religious institutions, although some secular hospitals such as Les invalides in Paris (for old and sick former military personnel) were founded and funded by monarchs.

Surgery was embryonic, and most surgical operations were about amputations, mending broken bones and removing stones from kidneys.

At the time, there was no regulation of the medical profession and most of the care provided was in the home, or at monasteries and nunneries, by non-professionals with limited knowledge of the human body (nuns, healers, midwives who acted from experience rather than science).

There were very few professional doctors. Barbers very often acted in the capacity of doctors and dentists.

The practice of bleeding, and applying leeches and suction cups as a remedy, was widespread, which in many cases made things worse.

Hygiene was rudimentary, and authorities did not know how to deal with epidemics or pandemics (such as the Great London Plague in 1665-66, which killed an estimated 100,000 people). However, there were some significant medical discoveries in that century. In 1628 in England, William Harvey explained blood circulation in his work *Exercitatio Anatomica de Motu Cordis et Sanguinis in Animalibus*, and in the 1670s, Antonie Philips van Leeuwenhoek, a Dutchman, invented the modern microscope with lenses that made it possible to observe unicellular organisms.

9

**Please turn over and spot 20 mistakes**

# In a
# 17th century hospital

## Key

1- Frankenstein's creature in a bed
2- Lollipops
3- The Caduceus, the symbol of medicine, has a salamander instead of two snakes in it
4- A jar of aspirin (a drug that was developed much later, in 1897)
5- An Emergency sign
6- A patient doing an X-ray (the first was performed in 1895)
7- A man with a pig's head
8- Toilet plungers instead of suction cups on the sick man's back
9- Monks performing a postmortem
10- A stethoscope (this instrument was invented by Laennec in 1816 to listen to heartbeats)
11- Saint Sebastian with his halo and body shot with arrows
12- A psychoanalyst giving a consultation (psychoanalysis was invented in the 19th Century)
13- Piranhas instead of leeches on the patient's back

14- A doctor using acupuncture (a branch of Chinese medicine which consists in planting needles at precise points in the body to treat the patient)
15- The anaesthetist (a doctor in charge of putting patients to sleep) uses a huge mallet
16- A sedan chair with a blue light on it
17- The vaccine against rabies (first experimented by Pasteur on a child in 1881)
18- A state-of-the-art microscope in the hands of Van Leeuwenhoek, a Dutchman who devised the first microscope in 1683
19- A modern surgery room
20- An arm being stitched with a sewing-machine.

# Restoring the
# Great Sphinx of Giza
## (1925-36)

The Great Sphinx of Giza has been a symbol of Egypt from ancient times to the present. It has inspired the imaginations of artists, poets, adventurers, scholars and travelers for centuries and has also inspired endless speculation about its age, its meaning and the secrets that it might hold.

It is an immense stone sculpture of a creature with the body of a lion and the head of a human. The greatest monumental sculpture in the ancient world, it is carved out of a single ridge of limestone 240 feet (73 meters) long and 66 feet (20 meters) high. The Sphinx sits in a shallow depression to the south of the pyramid of the Pharaoh Khafre (also known as Chephren) at the west bank of the Nile River near the city of Cairo.

According to traditional Egyptology the Sphinx was constructed in the 4th Dynasty (2575 – 2467 BCE) by the Pharaoh Khafre. However, some archeologists using geology suggest that the Sphinx is far older than the 4th Dynasty and was only restored by Khafre during his reign.

The purpose of the Sphinx is not known. Some orthodox archaeologists assume that it was a memorial to a Pharaoh or that it functioned as some sort of talisman or guardian deity.

Other scholars, however, believe the Sphinx functioned as an astronomical observation device that marked the position of the rising sun on the day of the spring equinox.

In 1798, when Napoleon came to Egypt the Sphinx was buried in sand up to its neck. Finally, between 1925 and 1936, the French engineer Emil Baraize was successful in clearing the sand to reveal the base of the Sphinx.

(13)

Please turn over and spot 19 mistakes

15

# Great Sphinx of Giza (1925-36)

## Key

1- The Statue of Liberty (it was inaugurated in New York Harbour in 1886)

2- The Sphinx wears an earring

3- A TV aerial at the top of a pyramid

4- An Aztec statue (Aztecs were a people who lived in Mexico between the 11th and the 16th centuries)

5- Anubis, the Egyptian god of mummification with a jackal's head, climbs a ladder

6- An umbrella

7- A pneumatic drill

8- A Chinese sign

9- A door on the sphinx

10- An excavator

11- A metal detector

12- A diver

13- A sarcophagus with a snorkel

14- A mummy among the workmen

15- The Easter Island statue (the monumental statues on Easter Island were sculpted between the 11th and the 15th centuries)

16- The flying saucer

17- The 'toilets' sign

18- The high-pressure washer

19- The Chinese statue (7000 such terracotta statues dating from the 3rd century BC were found in Lintong, China, in 1974)

# Gulliver and the Lilliputians

## Inspired by
## Jonathan Swift's Gulliver's Travels
## (1726).

Jonathan Swift (1667–1745) was an Anglo-Irish satirist, essayist, political pamphleteer, poet and cleric who became Dean of St Patrick's Cathedral, Dublin.

Swift is remembered for works such as Gulliver's Travels, A Modest Proposal, and A Tale of a Tub. He is regarded by the Encyclopædia Britannica as the foremost prose satirist in the English language. Gulliver's travels, a novel first published in 1726, is a satire of human nature and of the fanciful travel accounts that were common in Swift's time.

The book is divided into four sections, the most famous of which is the first one, which recounts his adventures in Lilliput : During his first voyage, Gulliver is washed ashore after a shipwreck and finds himself a prisoner of a race of tiny people, less than 6 inches tall, who are inhabitants of the island country of Lilliput.

After giving assurances of his good behaviour, he is given a residence in Lilliput and becomes a favourite of the Lilliput Court. He is also given permission to go around the city on condition that he must not harm their subjects.

At first, the Lilliputians are hospitable to Gulliver, but they are also wary of the threat that his size poses to them. Gulliver assists the Lilliputians to subdue their neighbours, the Blefuscudians, by stealing their fleet. Get a copy of the book and read the rest, you will enjoy it.

17

Please turn over and spot 21 mistakes

## Gulliver and the Lilliputians
### Inspired by Jonathan Swift's Gulliver's Travels (1726).

# Key

1- A plane (The first plane, dubbed Eole, was flown for the first time by Frenchman Clément Ader in 1890)

2- A hot-air balloon (The first hot-air balloon flight took place in 1783)

3- A boat anchor

4- The European Union flag

5- A flashlight

6- The Eiffel Tower

7- A camera

8- A fountain pen

9- A safety pin in Gulliver's ear (those were invented in 1849)

10- A moped

11- A wrist watch

12- A megaphone

13- A matchbox (matches were not produced until 1830)

14- A crush barrier

15- Two men pulling the same rope in opposite directions

16- A man wearing jeans, a tie and a bowler hat

17- A cell phone

18- A stethoscope

19- A Samurai sword

20- A radio cassette recorder (1970)

21- A 50-euro bill

# The First Games
# in Olympia

The Olympic Games were a series of athletic competitions among representatives of city-states of Ancient Greece.

They were held in honor of Zeus, and the Greeks gave them a mythological origin.

The first Olympics is traditionally dated to 776 BC. The games were held every four years, or olympiad, which became a unit of time in historical chronologies.

During the celebration of the games, an Olympic Truce was enacted so that athletes could travel from their cities to the games in safety.

The prizes for the victors were olive leaf wreaths or crowns. The ancient Olympics had fewer events than the modern games.

They comprised running, jumping, discus throw, wrestling, boxing, Pankration ( a primitive form of martial art combining wrestling and boxing) and equestrian events which included horse races and chariot races and took place in the Hippodrome, a wide, flat, open space.

Only freeborn Greek men were allowed to participate and attend. The games were always held at Olympia rather than moving between different locations as is the practice with the modern Olympic Games.

Victors at the Olympics were honored, and their feats chronicled for future generations

21

Please turn over and spot 20 mistakes

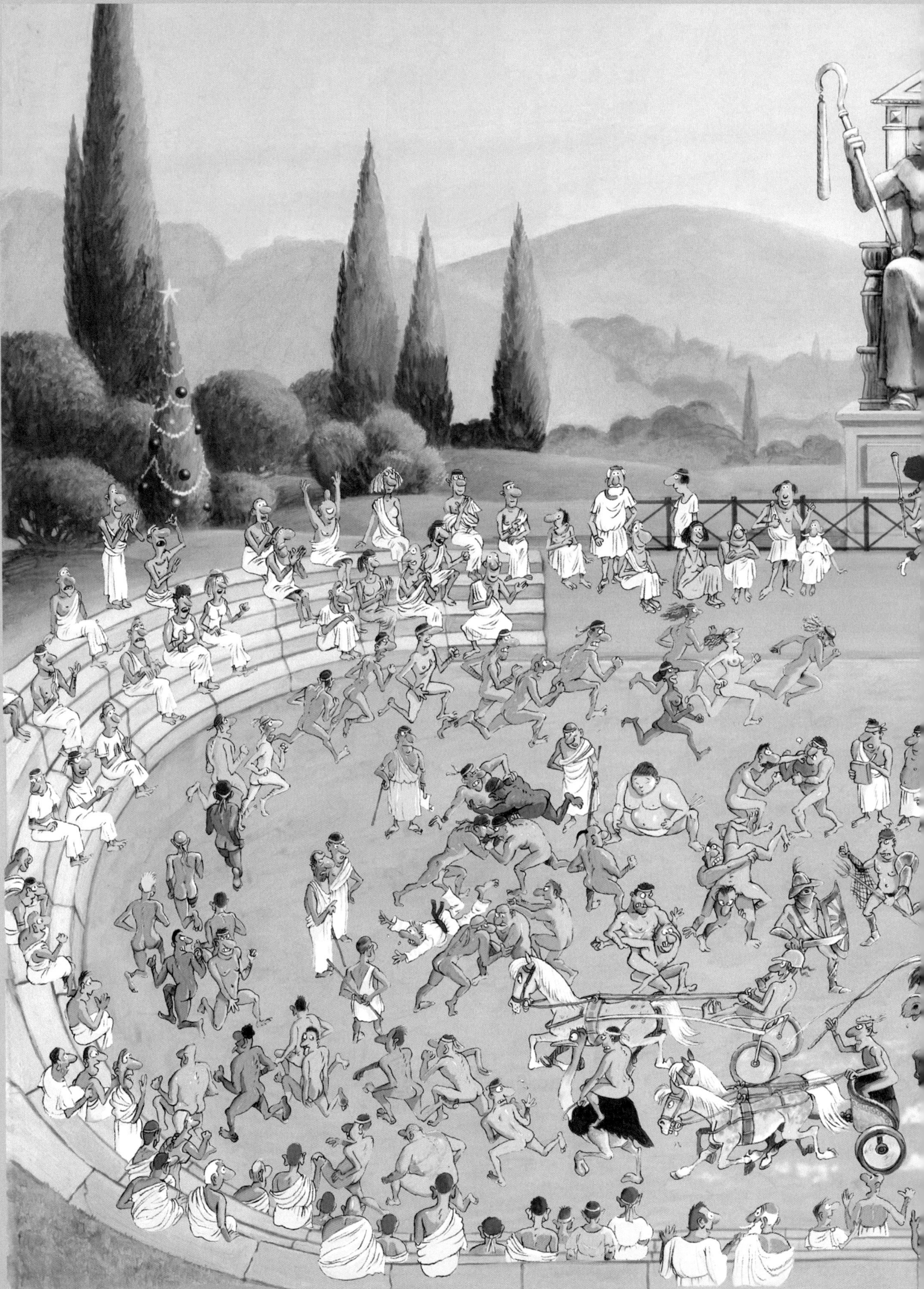

# The First Games in Olympia
## Key

1- A flail in Zeus's right hand

2- A balloon launch

3- Christmas decorations

4- Cheerleaders

5- There are women among the public and athletes (women were not admitted to the games)

6- Red Cross volunteers

7- Modern starting-blocks

8- A starting pistol

9- A boomerang

10- A sumo wrestler (Japanese)

11- Athletes are carrying a pillar

12- A chariot racer with a carrot hanging from a fishing-rod to get his horses running

13- A sprinter running in the wrong direction

14- A judoka (Judo is a martial art originating in Japan)

15- Roman gladiators

16- A man riding an ostrich

17- A sulky (a modern lightweight cart used for harness races)

18- A chariot racer using a whisk instead of a whip

19- A chariot with tyres

20- A chariot pulled by men and driven by a horse

# At the Mariinsky Theatre in St Petersburg
# Tsar Nicholas II of Russia
## attends a performance in 1916

Tsar Nicholas II or Nikolai II (1868-1918) was the last Emperor of Russia, ruling from 1 November 1894 until his forced abdication on 15 March 1917. His reign saw the fall of the Russian Empire from being one of the foremost great powers of the world to economic and military collapse. As head of state, Nicholas approved the Russian mobilization on 31 July 1914, which led to Germany declaring war on Russia on the following day. It is estimated that around 3.3 million Russians were killed in World War I.

The Imperial Army's severe losses and the High Command's incompetent management of the war efforts, along with the lack of food and other supplies on the Home Front, were the leading causes of the fall of the Romanov dynasty.

Following the February Revolution of 1917 Nicholas abdicated on behalf of himself and his son, and he and his family were imprisoned. In the spring of 1918, Nicholas was handed over to the local Ural Soviet; with the approval of Lenin, Nicholas and his family were eventually executed by the Bolsheviks on the night of 16–17 July 1918. The recovered remains of the Imperial Family were finally re-interred in St. Petersburg in 1998.

The Mariinsky Theatre is a historic theatre of opera and ballet in Saint Petersburg, Russia. Opened in 1860, it became the preeminent music theatre of late 19th century Russia, where many of the stage masterpieces of Tchaikovsky, Mussorgsky and Rimsky-Korsakov received their premieres.

Today, the Mariinsky Theatre is home to the Mariinsky Ballet, Mariinsky Opera and Mariinsky Orchestra. Since Yuri Temirkanov's retirement in 1988, the conductor Valery Gergiev has served as the theatre's general director.

(25)

**Please turn over and spot 18 mistakes**

EMERGENCY EXIT

POP CORN

At the Mariinsky Theatre in St Petersburg
Tsar Nicholas II of Russia attends a performance in 1916

# Key

1- Prehistoric cave paintings on the ceiling

2- A trapeze artist

3- A 'no smoking' sign

4- An imaginary animal instead of the golden eagle, emblem of the tsars of Russia

5- A cameraman

6- A coat of arms with the Hammer and Sickle, emblem of the former USSR

7- An upside down statue

8- Chinese lanterns

9- A chimpanzee

10- A woman playing with a fishing-rod

11- "Emergency exit" signs

12- A fireman wearing modern gear

13- The headline on the Newspaper *The Pravda*, announcing the assassination of the Tsar whereas he is attending the performance : "Tsar Assassinated"
*The Pravda*, meaning The Truth in Russian, was founded in 1912 by workers in St Petersburg and became the official paper of the Communist Party from 1917.

14- A knight in armor

15- An usherette with a flashlight

16- A man drinking a milk-shake

17- An officer eating popcorn

18- A man typing on a PC

# On the Run

Skiing, or traveling over snow on skis, is proved to have been a human practice for at least 7,000 years. The earliest archaeological artefacts thought to be skis were found in Russia and date to 5000 BCE. Although modern skiing has evolved from beginnings in Scandinavia, 10,000-year-old wall paintings suggest use of skis in the Xinjiang region of China.

Originally purely utilitarian, starting in the mid-1800s skiing became a popular recreational activity and sport, becoming practiced in snow-covered regions world-wide, and providing crucial economic support to purpose-built ski resorts and communities.

The word ski comes from the Old Norse word "skíð" which means " stick of wood ". In other old Scandinavian languages the word " ski " refers to split wood. Skiing was originally a means of transport rather than a recreational activity. Skis were in regular use by Scandinavian farmers, hunters and warriors throughout the Middle Ages. There are records dating back to the 18th Century showing that skis were used in operations by the Swedish army ( skiers travelled as fast, or even faster than men on horseback on snowy terrain).

From the mid-19th Century skiing (together with other mountain sport like sledding and mountaineering) became popular with civilians (from the wealthier classes) who travelled to mountain areas for the purpose ; in the 20th Century it became more democratic, a sport and a recreation practised by millions of people worldwide, especially after World War II.

Alpine ( downhill) skiing, which involves ski-lifts and requires high mountains is more widespread than Nordic (cross-country) skiing, which can be practised everywhere, provided there is snow of course !

**Please turn over and spot 30 mistakes**

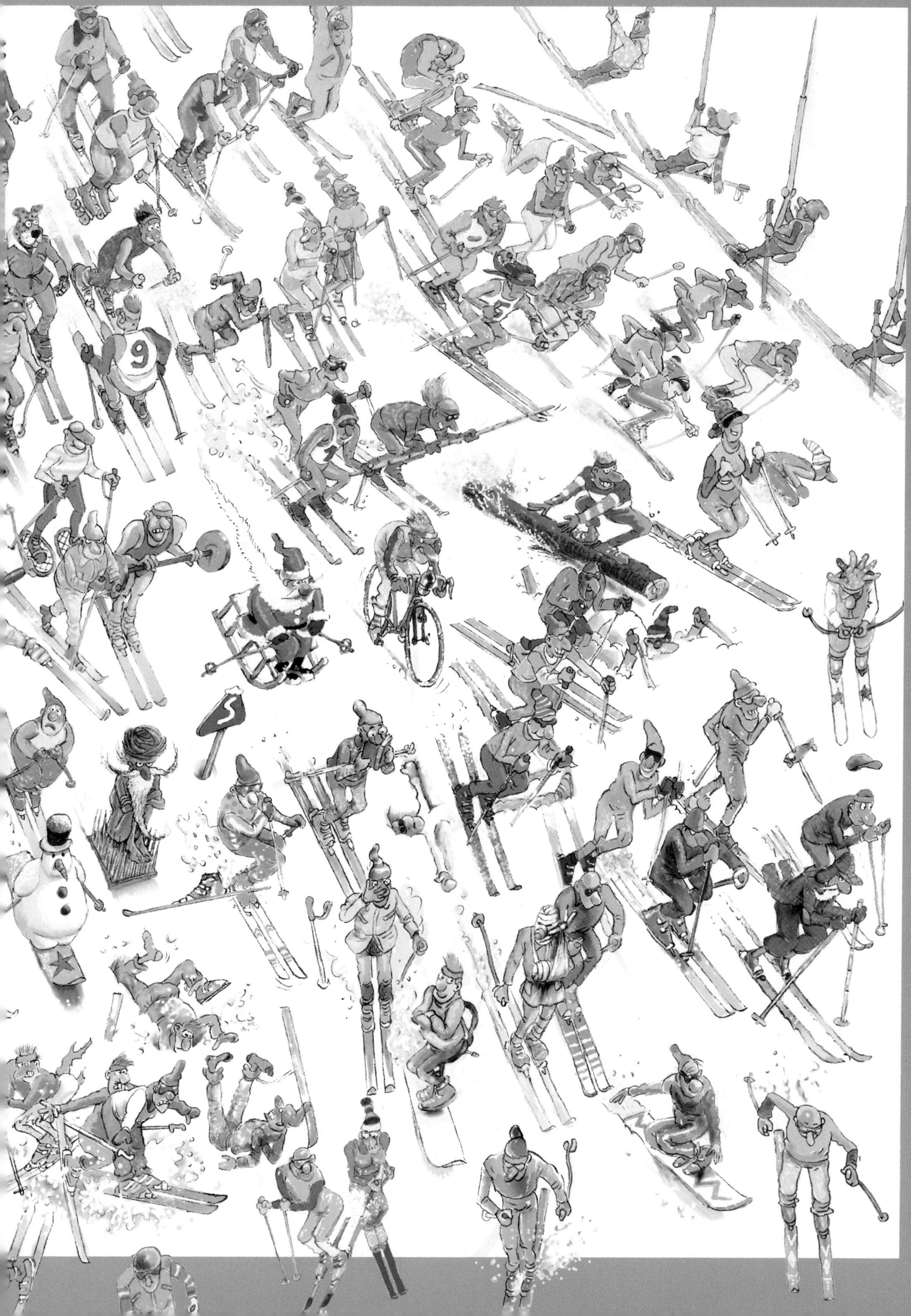

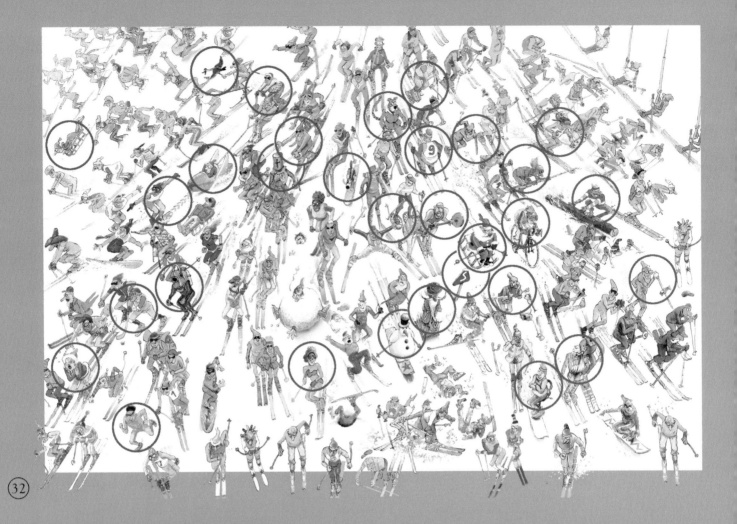

# On the Run

## key

1- An ice hockey player on a ski run

2- A diver

3- A skier towed by a duck

4- A skier with oars

5- A skier wearing jewellery gets robbed

6- A skier without skis

7- A water-skier towed by a fun-fair machine

8- A skier in armor

9- A woman in a bathing suit

10- A blind skier with a white cane

11- A leopard skier

12- A skier with snowshoes
   (which are normally used on fresh snow)

13- A snowman on skis

14- A skier on roller-skates

15- A skier skiing back to front

16- A weight-lifter on skis

17- A fakir skier on a bed of nails

18- A « bend ahead » roadsign

19- A skier has a French baguette for a pole

20- A skier is reading a book

21- A Santa on a sled (there are separate
   slopes for sleds)

22- A skier on a bar seat

23- A skier with a fishing-rod for a pole

24- A skier with a ski-lift pole instead
   of a regular pole

25- A cyclist

26- A blindfolded skier

27- A skier riding a log (like
   in Canadian log driving)

28- A skier bandaged up like a mummy

29- A skier with a fish harpooned on his pole

30- A snowmobile

# Hollywood 1933 :
# shooting the first
# King Kong film

King Kong is a 1933 American monster film directed and produced by Merian C. Cooper and Ernest B. Schoedsack.When it was released it instantly became a blockbuster ; today it is often ranked as one of the most famous horror films of all times.

King Kong is especially noted for the use of stop-motion animation with models. One Kong model was constructed on a one-inch-equals-one-foot scale to simulate a gorilla 18 feet tall. In all, four models were built: two jointed 18-inch aluminum, foam rubber, latex, and rabbit fur models, one jointed 24-inch model of the same materials for the New York scenes, and a small model of lead and fur for the tumbling -down-the-Empire-State-Building scene.

Besides, a huge bust of Kong's head, neck, and upper chest was made of wood, cloth, rubber, and bearskin. Inside the structure, metal levers, hinges, and an air compressor were operated by three men to control the mouth and facialexpressions. Its scale matched none of the models and, if fully realized, Kong would have stood thirty to forty feet tall.

Two versions of Kong's right hand and arm were constructed of steel, sponge rubber, rubber, and bearskin. The first hand was nonarticulated, mounted on a crane, and operated by grips for the scene in which Kong grabs at a character. The other hand and arm had articulated fingers, was mounted on a lever to elevate it, and was used in the several scenes in which Kong grasps his female "friend".

33

Please turn over and spot 20 mistakes

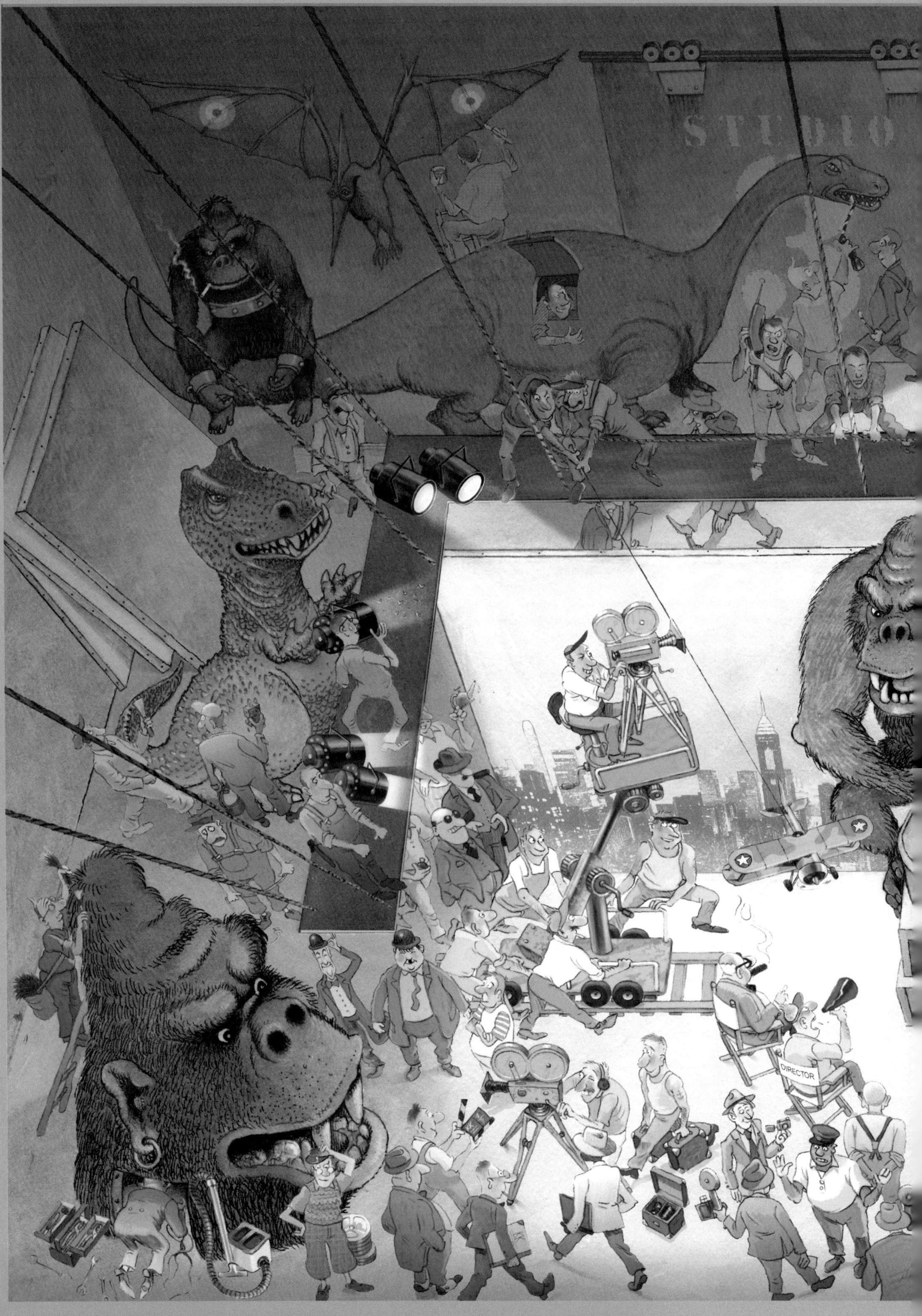
STUDIO
DIRECTOR

## Hollywood 1933 :
## shooting the first King Kong film
## Key

1- The King Kong puppet is smoking a cigarette

2- Roundels on the pterodactyl's wings

3- The dino (an animatronic) is drinking a coke

4- A walkie-talkie

5- A policeman is walking with a corded telephone

6- There is a Vespa scooter outside (those came out in the 50s)

7- A machinist is using a model boat instead of a model plane for the scene

8- Another machinist is using a remote control

9- Laurel & Hardy are out of place on the King Kong set

10- There is a modern « steadycam » on the set

11- Someone is painting the set with a paint roller

12- There is a chair for King Kong

13- Tarzan in King Kong's hand (this is a different movie!)

14- King Kong's hand has red nail varnish on one finger

15- The female star is in black and white

16- A photographer has got a small digital camera

17- A modern hoover

18- An ear piercing on the giant head

19- A poster of Marylin Monroe by Andy Warhol (1962)

20- A photographer is doing a selfie with the star.

# Back in the
## Old Stone Age

What is called the Stone Age was a time in prehistory when our ancestors made tools and weapons out of stone. It started about 3.4 million years ago, and lasted until the introduction of bronze tools, and then iron tools a few thousand years ago.

The Stone Age is divided into three periods according to the type of stone tools used, and the dates of these periods vary across the world.

The Old Stone (Paleolithic) Age lasted from the first use of stones until the end of the last Ice Age. The stone tools and weapons were then made of roughly chipped stone, and early humans were only hunters and gatherers.

In the Middle Stone (Mesolithic) Age, humans made finer chipped stone tools and started domesticating plants and animals. It lasted from the end of the last Ice Age until the start of farming.

The New Stone (Neolithic) Age lasted from the start of farming until the first use of metal. Stones were then polished. The term lithic comes from the Ancient Greek word for stone or rock.

**Please turn over and spot 30 mistakes**

## Back in the Old Stone Age

# Key

1- A woman is knitting a sock

2- A hairdresser's salon

3- A man teaching a group about the Circle (geometry was evolved much later)

4- A man carrying a basin and cooking pans

5- A pterodactyl (they were extinct)

6- A sword (from the Bronze Age)

7- A lighter

8- A wristwatch

9- A tatoo of a boat anchor

10- A plough

11- A cereal field (agriculture came much later)

12- Sickles (from the Iron Age)

13- A waste bin

14- Metal rungs on the rock

15- A car radio

16- A man painting Picasso's famous Bull Head

17- A painter's palette

18- Some feline footprints instead of men's hand prints

19- Scissors

20- A baby bottle

21- A pressure cooker

22- A letter and mailbox

23- A dinosaur (they were extinct)

24- A man fishing a shoe out of the water

25- A man sculpting a car

27- A small gas bottle

28- A camping tent

29- A Stairs/B Stairs written on the rock wall

30- A man reading a book

Coming soon

Spot the nonsense

2

# Acknowledgements

I am sincerely grateful to Wikipedia
for providing all the info we used in the
background texts. Please donate to Wikipedia !
   Thanks also to Albert Dubout, Gérard
Lauzier, Jean Louis Ginibre, Alain Lesault,
Bernard Giraudroux, Margarethe Hubauer,
who inspired me and helped me in
my career as a cartoonist
   On this particular volume, many thanks
to Christine for her initiatives and
tenaciousness, to Anne for her enthusiasm and
concise texts, and to the Amazon CreateSpace
team for making it all possible.


W/D. GUERRIER

CPSIA information can be obtained at www.ICGtesting.com
Printed in the USA
LVIW01n1450280917
550413LV00012B/137